From Idea to Publish

The Ultimate Author's Checklist to Write and
Publish a Non-Fiction Book

GRACE MARIE BROWN

ORDERING INFORMATION

Quantity sales. Special discounts are available on quantity purchases by corporations, associations, and others. For details, contact the publisher at contact@pentopublish.com

Printed in the United States of America

ISBN: 9781074175856

Established by Grace Marie Brown, International Ghostwriter & Book Coach, Pen to Publish is a brand committed to helping DIY authors write and self-publish like a pro. We offer online classes, workshops, resources, coaching, and services designed to meet the needs of aspiring and current authors.

Visit our website to access our suite of learning resources and schedule a free consultation to discuss our services.

Email: contact@pentopublish.com
Website: www.pentopublish.com
Facebook: @pentopublish

Introduction

You Are on Your Way to Becoming a Self-Published Author

As a ghostwriter and book coach, I cannot tell you how often I hear these questions - *"Where do I start?" "So, what's next?"* If you are writing your book for the first time, there is no way for you to know all that it takes to get you from the idea you have in your head to the self-published author with a print book in hand.

In many instances, a first-time author may not even know where to start, much less to fully comprehend what to do at each stage of the self-publishing journey. *This checklist will help you!*

After ghostwriting more than 200 books, publishing 8 of my own, and coaching hundreds of individuals to self-published status, I have decided to share my checklist for my book projects and those of my clients.

Just as how you need some navigation assistance when going to a new location, so it is with writing your book — especially if it is your first time. So, consider this checklist your GPS to writing and publishing your book. You could try to get there without it, but it just makes sense to turn on the GPS and avoid the uncertainty.

Each checklist item will take you one step closer to self-publishing success.

I have also included some of my pro tips, resources that you can use to write and publish your book, and a 12-week planner to guide you along the way. The planner will help complete the weekly tasks as assigned.

Writing and publishing success requires work and you will have to invest the time necessary to execute the tasks it will take to get you *From Idea to Publish*. This checklist is not written as a manual, but each checklist item will give you clarity on what you should be doing as you work on your book. Each section of the checklist includes a section to take notes.

I know you have a burning desire to write your book. It is time to get it done. Use this checklist as your guiding tool as you embark upon this journey.

I look forward to your success. And I know you got this.

Grace Marie Brown
International Ghostwriter & Book Coach

Self-Publishing Explained

For a long time, if an author wanted to self-publish, they had to invest thousands of dollars with what is referred to as a "vanity" press. In most instances, an author would have to come out of pocket to buy a large amount of their book and pray that they can sell them all.

However, with the advent of print-on-demand (POD) technology and self-publishing platforms like KDP, self-publishing is now accessible to anyone wanting to write a book. POD allows books to be printed one at a time and when demanded. Today, self-publishing authors don't have to have a deep pocket to get their book in the hands of their readers.

How does it work? When you write and upload your book to a platform like KDP; they will distribute your book to websites like Amazon and Barnes and

Nobles. When a reader wants to buy your book, they order it from Amazon; the book is printed and delivered to the reader. In return, both Amazon and KDP gets a cut and you get paid royalties.

If as an author, you want to buy books to sell at an event or on your website, you can order author's copies at printing cost; which can be as low as $2.15.

There are two ways to self-publish in today's market.

1. Self-publish completely on your own, only outsourcing to freelancers to assist with specific tasks.

2. Self-publish by hiring a service company to carry out publishing steps.

Hiring a Self-Publish Service Company

Many authors use this method because all they have to do is write a check and let someone else deal with the headache. If you have more money than time, then this is the best option for you.

Self-publishing companies all have different terms

of engagement, but all charge an upfront fee, and usually own no rights to the book. They make money by charging authors for the services provided (editing, formatting, book cover design, and uploading).

The benefit is that you get a published book without having to figure out the details and technicalities of the publishing industry.

DIY Self-Publishing

Today, anyone can get access to the same level of online retail distribution as a traditional publisher, by using platforms like KDP. There are no upfront fees and KDP will publish and distribute your book.

As the author, you do all the heavy lifting, such as editing, formatting, and book cover design. The alternative is to outsource these tasks to freelancers. With DIY self-publishing you take on all the headache, but you can do it on a low budget.

With self-publishing, you take control and become your own publisher!

Outsourcing

When I wrote my first book, I did it all. Back then I knew very little about publishing and I just wanted to write and finish my book. It was truly a learning experience, but it was also riddled with mistakes. Today, even with years of experience and expertise, there are some areas of my personal projects that I outsource.

As a DIY author, you will have to understand your strengths and weakness and outsource to others the tasks that fall under the latter. Additionally, if you are busy and have the budget, outsourcing will free up time to do other things.

Hiring a Book Coach

A book coach is someone who can guide you through the process of writing and publishing your book. They act as a handholding and accountability partner. But even more so, you get access to their expertise in self-publishing so that you can avoid the mistakes and pitfalls along the way.

Hiring a Ghostwriter

A hired professional writer, ghostwriters have been around for as long as books have been in print. They will work with you to develop the content for your book and carry out the heavy lifting of writing your manuscript.

In the list of outsourcing professionals, they will be the most expensive. Authors who are busy or who find it hard to express themselves in writing will often seek out a ghostwriter.

Ghostwriters often do not need credit. They are bound by a confidentiality agreement and do not claim any rights to the finished book unless mutually agreed upon.

As a ghostwriter, I explain to my clients that I write it, but they own it.

Hiring a Virtual Assistant

Virtual assistants can be helpful to authors. They are normally contracted to hire and manage freelancers, answer emails, keep the author on track, do research, help with the launch, amongst other things.

You can find several affordable assistants on freelancer websites like Fiverr or Upwork.

Hiring an Editor

If nothing else, you should invest in an editor. Professional editing is critical to the success of your book.

Editors are to be differentiated from proof-readers. The latter is concerned with fixing critical grammatical mistakes, but do not focus on readability, flow, and other advanced technical issues. You want a copy editor to complete thorough edits of your manuscript.

This can be an expensive service, but worth it.

Hiring a Graphic Designer

A graphic designer is going to help you bring the vision of your book cover to reality. This is an important hire as we know that readers will judge your book by the cover.

You want to hire someone with experience and a large portfolio. The graphic designer of choice should also be aware of the submission guidelines of your self-publishing platform of choice. You can find several great graphic designers on freelancer websites like Fivver and Upwork.

Hiring a Self-Publishing Company

A self-publishing company normally takes on the editing, formatting, cover design, and uploading of your book. This can be helpful; instead of hiring several individuals, you hire one person or company to do it all.

Prices for this service will vary and it is important to do your research before your sign on the dotted line.

Outsourcing has its pros and cons. But when you find the right people, you can alleviate a lot of the headaches and give you more time to spend on other areas of your book project.

Plan Your Book

The biggest mistake an author can make is to start writing a book without a plan. This section of the checklist will outline the steps to planning your book project.

Gain Clarity

☐ Choose the niche topic for your book. Consider a topic that you have specific knowledge of, is passionate about, and one that sells.

☐ Figure out what you want your readers to get from your book. What's in it for them?

☐ Establish what you, your business, or brand will gain from writing this book. What is the real reason behind writing this book?

☐ Define your target audience and/or who should read your book. Be specific in describing the ideal reader for your book.

☐ Carry out the market research of your niche category. You want to know what your ideal reader wants, what's currently being offered and how you can fill a gap.

Pro Tip: You might have several book ideas. Choose the book that you know you can sell to your current audience. This way you have a willing and able customer base.

Notes

_____

_____

_____

_____

_____

_____

_____

_____

_____

_____

_____

_____

_____

_____

_____

_____

Draft book details

- ☐ Brainstorm and settle on the main title for your book. Make sure it is something that is attention-grabbing.

- ☐ Brainstorm and settle on a sub-title that will explain what the book is about.

- ☐ Decide if you will use a pen name and what it will be. This optionally, but if you choose to use one, make sure you research the legality of doing so.

- ☐ Determine if your book will be print, ebook, or both. You might also be interested in doing an audiobook.

- ☐ Prepare a short description of your book or elevator pitch that will tell readers and others what you book is about and why they should read it.

Pro Tip: Before deciding on a title, search Amazon to make sure you have a unique Title. While an author cannot copyright the title of a book, having a book with the same title as another book can drive traffic away from your book.

Notes

_____

_____

_____

_____

_____

_____

_____

_____

_____

_____

_____

_____

_____

_____

_____

_____

_____

_____

_____

_____

_____

_____

Establish a writing plan

☐ Determine an estimated word or page count for your book.

☐ Figure out how you will develop the content of the book and where it will come from.

☐ Prepare a detailed book outline, mapping out the content for your introduction and the chapters for your book.

☐ Create a daily writing schedule to help you keep on track and finish your book project.

Pro Tip: If you want a print book of 100+ pages, then you need content totaling 20k to 25k words.

Notes

_____

_____

_____

_____

_____

_____

_____

_____

_____

_____

_____

_____

_____

_____

_____

_____

_____

_____

_____

_____

_____

Consider your publishing plan

☐ Decide on your self-publishing platform of choice for uploading your book.

☐ Write down your vision for the design of your book cover.

☐ Evaluate your ISBN options and decide whether to buy or get a free ISBN.

☐ Research and determine your book printing options.

Pro Tip: KDP is by far the #1 self-publishing platform for DIY authors. Upload your manuscript and cover and KDP will publish your book to Amazon and other distribution channels. You can also order printed copies of your book to sell at events or on your website.

Notes

_____

_____

_____

_____

_____

_____

_____

_____

_____

_____

_____

_____

_____

_____

_____

_____

_____

_____

_____

_____

_____

_____

_____

_____

_____

Put together a marketing plan

- ☐ Prepare a plan of action for an online and offline book launch

- ☐ Determine the digital marketing strategies you will use to promote your book online.

- ☐ Determine offline marketing strategies you will use to promote your book at events and in stores.

- ☐ Plan daily marketing activities for the first 30 days of being published

Pro Tip: Your book is a product and just like any other product, you must market it to your target audience. Consider marketing in Facebook groups and email marketing. For offline marketing consider events and vendor opportunities.

Notes

_____

_____

_____

_____

_____

_____

_____

_____

_____

_____

_____

_____

_____

_____

_____

_____

_____

_____

Brainstorm funding

☐ Construct an expense list to write and publish your book.

☐ Research costs for each item on the expense list.

☐ Determine your available sources of funding to meet the expenses.

☐ Create a book writing and publishing budget.

Pro Tip: When you have a limited budget consider making your book available for pre-order. You will need to have a book cover design, a platform to receive payments, and commitment to a launch date.

Notes

_____

_____

_____

_____

_____

_____

_____

_____

_____

_____

_____

_____

_____

_____

_____

_____

_____

_____

_____

_____

_____

_____

_____

_____

_____

_____

Book planning can seem boring to many aspiring authors, but it critical to your writing and publishing success. Write down your plan and refer to it as you go through the publishing process.

If you are struggling with putting a plan together, consider hiring a coach to help you gain clarity and complete your plan.

Write Your Book

Now that you have a plan in place, it is time to move to the next step — writing. This section of the checklist will help you execute your writing plan.

Get into the zone

- ☐ Identify a comfortable writing space that is free from distractions.

- ☐ Get support from those close to you to help as execute your plan to write and publish your book.

- ☐ Incorporate motivational and accountability measures that will keep you focused and on task.

Pro Tip: Sometimes you have to get away from all the distractions. Schedule a writing weekend at a hotel or Airbnb and focus on writing your book.

Notes

_____

_____

_____

_____

_____

_____

_____

_____

_____

_____

_____

_____

_____

_____

_____

_____

_____

_____

_____

_____

Implement your writing plan

☐ Gather previously recorded or written content that will be used in your book.

☐ Review your book outline and make amendments if necessary.

☐ Conduct interviews with and collect content from contributors to the book if part of your book plan.

☐ Include writing schedule in your day to day planning.

Pro Tip: Try to schedule 1 hour per day to work on your book. You can wake up 30 minutes earlier and go to bed 30 minutes later

Notes

_____

_____

_____

_____

_____

_____

_____

_____

_____

_____

_____

_____

_____

_____

_____

_____

_____

_____

_____

_____

Just write

☐ Write the introduction

☐ Write the chapters

☐ Write the concluding chapter

☐ Incorporate contributing content obtained from interviews or other sources if part of your writing plan.

Pro Tip: If you are struggling with expressing yourself in writing, try speaking your book by recording what you want to say and get the audio transcribed.

Notes

_____
_____
_____
_____
_____
_____
_____
_____
_____
_____
_____
_____
_____
_____
_____
_____
_____
_____

Analyze Content

☐ Review your first draft to fill in gaps and add more content where necessary.

☐ Review your first draft to remove redundant information from your manuscript.

☐ Verify the accuracy of quotes or content obtained from other sources.

Pro Tip: Take a mental break before analyzing the content of your first draft. This will give you time to approach the content with a fresh mind.

Notes

_____

_____

_____

_____

_____

_____

_____

_____

_____

_____

_____

_____

_____

_____

_____

_____

_____

_____

Prepare front and back of book content

☐ Write copyright page content

☐ Draft a table of content if needed.

☐ Write dedication page if needed

☐ Write acknowledgment page if needed

☐ Write foreword if needed

☐ Write an "about the author" page

☐ Write resource or additional information page if needed.

Pro Tip: Not sure what content to include in the front and back of your book? Take a visit to a bookstore and look at other books. What you include will come down to preference.

Notes

_____

_____

_____

_____

_____

_____

_____

_____

_____

_____

_____

_____

_____

_____

_____

_____

_____

_____

_____

_____

The writing process can be long and this where a lot of aspiring authors give. Stay the course and if you are having difficulties expressing yourself in writing, then consider hiring a ghostwriter.

Edit Your Book

Now that the hard work is over, get ready for more hard work. This section of the checklist will give you the steps you need to take to rid your manuscript of grammatical and technical writing issues.

First round of edits

☐ Read through entire book silently (in your mind).

☐ Fix obvious grammatical errors as you read through your manuscript.

☐ Incorporate corrections suggested by Word that do not alter the meaning of your content.

Pro Tip: You will not catch all the errors in your first round of edits. If you are self-editing focus on the obvious errors in the first round.

Notes

_____

_____

_____

_____

_____

_____

_____

_____

_____

_____

_____

_____

_____

_____

_____

_____

_____

_____

_____

Second round of edits

☐ Read through entire book aloud.

☐ Fix inconsistencies, flow, and readability issues as you read through the manuscript.

☐ Finalize chapter, sections, and paragraph heading in this round of edits.

Pro Tip: Sub-headings are not mandatory, but they help organize the content for you and the reader.

Notes

_____

_____

_____

_____

_____

_____

_____

_____

_____

_____

_____

_____

_____

_____

_____

_____

_____

_____

Third round of edits

☐ Read through the entire book with Grammarly or another artificial intelligence editing software.

☐ Fix suggested critical and advanced issues not previously identified.

☐ Ignore suggestions that alter the intent of your content

Pro Tip: There is a free version to Grammarly that you can install in word. This version will suggest critical grammatical errors.

Notes

_____

_____

_____

_____

_____

_____

_____

_____

_____

_____

_____

_____

_____

_____

_____

Final round of edits

- ☐ Read through the entire book with the text to speech add-on in Word (Speak).

- ☐ Ask a friend or family member to offer a second pair of eyes to proofread the manuscript.

- ☐ Consider if you need a copy editor to fix advanced issues.

Pro Tip: If you are using a friend or family member to help edit, let them know that you want their critical opinion and not just a reader.

Notes

_____

_____

_____

Editing your manuscript gets you one step closer to being ready to publish. However, it can be a very tedious process and if it is not your strength then consider outsourcing this task to a copy editor.

Format Your Book

Once the content of your manuscript is completed, the next step is to design the interior layout of the book. This section of the checklist will show you the steps you need to take to format your manuscript.

Pre-formatting tasks

☐ Finalize the self-publishing platform you plan on using to upload and distribute your book.

☐ Familiarize yourself with the platform's publishing and upload requirements.

☐ Finalize the trim size you want for your book.

☐ Download the classic book template from www.pentopublish.com and familiarize yourself with the interior submission guidelines of your self-publishing platform of choice.

Pro Tip: The preferred trim size for most non-fiction book is 6x9.

Notes

_____

_____

_____

_____

_____

_____

_____

_____

_____

_____

_____

_____

_____

_____

_____

_____

_____

Arrange content

- ☐ Import/paste introduction and chapter content to the template
- ☐ Import/paste front of book content to the template

☐ Import/paste back of book content to the template

☐ Replace title and copyright page template content with yours

☐ Replace page header and footer content with yours

☐ Delete any excess "sample" content in the template

Pro Tip: Save your formatted template with a different file name. This way if you make any mistakes while formatted you can also revert to your file with your draft.

Notes

_____

_____

_____

_____

_____

_____

_____
_____
_____
_____
_____
_____
_____
_____
_____
_____
_____
_____
_____
_____

Make important formatting adjustments

☐ Adjust font type and size to your preference

☐ Adjust line and paragraph spacing to your preference.

☐ Ensure that there are page breaks after each chapter and after each front of book section.

☐ Check to make sure that pictures and tables are within the print area

Pro Tip: If using pictures in your manuscript, check interiors submission guidelines of your publishing platform.

Notes

Add personal touch

☐ Insert chapter heading separator if needed

☐ Include drop letters if needed

☐ Include watermark or other graphics options if needed

Pro Tip: Some formatting features will be based on personal preference. Look at other books and determine what you want to add to enhance the visual presentation of your book.

Notes

_____

_____

_____

_____

_____

_____

_____

_____

_____

_____

_____

_____

_____

_____

_____

_____

_____

Final formatting checks

☐ Check for formatting consistency with font type and size.

☐ Check for blank pages and inconsistent spacing between paragraphs.

☐ Include page references for the table of content if there is one.

☐ Obtain ISBN and include it on the copyright page.

☐ Do one final read-through of the formatted book.

Pro Tip: If you want to use the free ISBN from KDP, you will have to start the book set up on your dashboard. The ISBN will be assigned before you upload the manuscript. Copy and paste the ISBN number and add it to your copyright page before uploading the file.

Notes

_____

_____

_____

_____

_____

_____

_____

_____

_____

_____

_____

_____

_____

_____

_____

_____

_____

_____

_____

Like editing, formatting can also be tedious. Using a pre-formatted template will save you time and headache as a DIY author.

Book Cover Design

The old saying "never judge a book by its cover" is far from true when self-publishing your book. In this section of the checklist find out about the steps you need to take to design your book cover.

Gain clarity

☐ Research other book covers in your niche category.

☐ Put together examples of cover designs that you like.

☐ Determine book cover imagery preference to you would like to include in your design.

☐ Determine book cover color preferences base on the target audience and/or your brand.

☐ Draw or design a mock-up of the book cover if possible.

Pro Tip: Do not underestimate the power of colors. Research color options and how each color conveys a different message to your target audience.

Notes

_____
_____
_____
_____
_____
_____
_____
_____
_____
_____
_____
_____
_____
_____
_____
_____
_____
_____
_____
_____
_____
_____

Develop book cover content

- ☐ Open a document to prepare book cover content

- ☐ Include title, subtitle and author name

- ☐ Prepare any other front book cover content needed

- ☐ Prepare content for back of book cover

- ☐ Determine and write what will be included as spine content

Pro Tip: Journal and notebooks generally carry limited back of book content while memoirs and informational books include more information about the book and the author.

Notes

_____

_____

_____

_____

_____

_____
_____
_____
_____
_____
_____
_____
_____
_____
_____
_____
_____
_____
_____
_____
_____
_____

Hire graphic designer

☐ Research possible graphic designers with book cover design experience

☐ Sign contract or agree to the terms and conditions to design cover

☐ Provide the designer with examples, color and imagery preference, and if available a mockup.

☐ Provide the designer with book cover content, publishing platform trims size, and page count for the book.

Pro Tip: The terms of your contract with a graphic designer should include that the designer will fix any cover issues identified by KDP or your publishing platform and to do so at no extra cost.

Notes

_____

_____

_____

_____

_____

_____

_____

_____

_____

_____

_____

_____

_____

Manage the design process

☐ Request more than one design options if included in the contract.

☐ Review the first draft and make suggested revisions to design concept.

☐ Review the second draft for accuracy of revision and content.

☐ Get a second or third opinion from a friend/family/other before finalizing .

Pro Tip: Not sure what design to choose? Then get your audience involved and let them vote on the design they prefer.

Notes

_____

_____

_____

_____

_____

_____

_____

_____

_____

_____

_____

_____

_____

_____

_____

Finalize cover

☐ Use zoom in feature to review the final draft

☐ Double check the book cover content for grammar or other issues.

☐ Request jpeg and PDF versions of book cover design.

☐ Request ebook version of book cover design.

Pro Tip: Your print cover must be a PDF document if you are publishing with KDP. For the ebook that design can be a jpeg. Check the file submission requirements for your publishing platform.

Notes

This is by far one of the most exciting stages of publishing your book. It is important to create a book cover that will grab the attention of your audience. While you can DIY your book cover, if creativity is not one of your strengths then it might be best to outsource.

Publish Your Book

Now that you have completed both the interior and the exterior of your book, you are now on your way to the final step in this checklist — publishing your book.

Pre-upload activities

☐ Create an account for the preferred self-publishing platform.

☐ Convert print book manuscript to pdf.

☐ Finalize book cover type and binding.

☐ Start planning your launch or implementing your launch plan

Pro Tip: Most self-publishing platforms will ask that the manuscript be uploaded as a PDF. If you formatted your book in word, there is a feature that allows you to export the file as a PDF.

Notes

_____

_____

_____

_____

_____

_____

_____

_____

_____

_____

_____

_____

_____

_____

_____

_____

_____

Prepare publishing content

☐ Prepare or finalize book description

☐ Research and write out the best SEO keywords for your book.

☐ Research and write out preferred search categories for the placement of your book.

Pro Tip: Search Amazon for books on the same or similar topic of your book. Look at their category placement and determine which of those categories best fit with your book.

Notes

_____

_____

_____

_____

_____

_____

_____

_____

_____

_____

_____

_____

_____

_____

_____

_____

_____

_____

_____

_____

Upload book

☐ Follow upload instructions from the publishing platform of choice.

☐ Double check to make sure that the right manuscript and book cover files are uploaded.

☐ Submit files for review.

☐ Make adjustments to manuscript and book cover after review if needed.

Pro Tip: The digital proofing process is important. Review each page in the KDP previewer. The technology is not perfect and sometimes content will appear different from your word or PDF document.

Notes

_____

_____

_____

_____

_____

_____

_____

_____

_____

_____

_____

_____

_____

_____

_____

_____

_____

_____

Manage the proofing process

☐ Review digital proof of the book for shifting of content or other errors after review.

☐ Request physical proof copy of your book.

☐ Review physical proof copy for any issues in the manuscript or on the book cover.

☐ Get a second opinion about the proof from a friend or family.

☐ Approve the book proof on your self-publishing platform and submit the book to be published.

☐ Wait the required time for the book to go live.

Pro Tip: Review the physical proof of your book with critical eyes. Do a full read-through of the book.

Notes

_____
_____
_____
_____
_____
_____
_____
_____
_____
_____
_____
_____
_____
_____
_____
_____

Set up your author's profile

- ☐ Create your author central account or the equivalent author profile account for your publishing platform.

- ☐ Prepare and upload your author's bio.

- ☐ Take and upload your author's picture.

- ☐ Include links to website, social media, or blog.

- ☐ Connect title to author's profile

Pro Tip: You will not be able to add your book to your author's profile until it is live on Amazon. Work on the other information for your profile and then add your book as soon as it goes live.

Notes

_____

_____

_____

_____

_____

_____
_____
_____
_____
_____
_____
_____
_____
_____
_____
_____

Finalize publishing

☐ Find book page on publishing platform or bookstore website.

☐ Check book page details for accuracy.

☐ Request or make changes where necessary.

☐ Create a short URL link or map long link to a domain name.

☐ Launch your book

Pro Tip: Sometimes your print and ebook may not be on the same page. Call KDP and make a request for the two titles to merge on the same Amazon page.

Notes

_____

_____

_____

_____

_____

_____

_____

_____

_____

_____

_____

_____

_____

_____

_____

_____

_____

_____

_____

_____

Congratulations, you've done it. It might have been a long process, but it is all worth it in the end. Now even more work begins as you now embark on the marketing and income generation activities for your book.

Planner

12-Week Planner

This 12-week planner is designed to help you stay on track to write and publish your book. It incorporates the steps from the checklist which are organized weekly so that you know what you should be doing each week.

How to use the planner

☐ Carry out the pre-determined to do activities and include any other activities you want.

☐ Use the notes section to record notes from any coaching, training, or research.

☐ Record your wins each week to keep you motivated.

☐ If the pre-determined activities are not completed carry them over to the next week.

Week 1

TO DO:

- ☐ Gain Clarity
- ☐ Draft Book Detail
- ☐ Establish Writing Plan

NOTES:

_____
_____
_____
_____
_____
_____
_____
_____
_____
_____
_____
_____
_____
_____
_____
_____
_____
_____
_____

GRACE MARIE BROWN

_____
_____
_____
_____
_____
_____
_____
_____
_____
_____
_____
_____
_____

WINS:

_____
_____
_____
_____
_____
_____
_____
_____
_____
_____
_____
_____
_____
_____

TO DO:

- ☐ Publishing Plan
- ☐ Prepare Marketing Plan
- ☐ Brainstorm Funding

NOTES:

_____

_____

_____

_____

_____

_____

_____

_____

_____

_____

_____

_____

_____

_____

_____

_____

_____

_____

_____

_____
_____
_____
_____
_____
_____
_____
_____
_____
_____
_____
_____
_____

WINS:

_____
_____
_____
_____
_____
_____
_____
_____
_____
_____
_____
_____

TO DO:

- ☐ Gather Info
- ☐ Research
- ☐ Review Outline

NOTES:

_____

_____

_____

_____

_____

_____

_____

_____

_____

_____

_____

_____

_____

_____

_____

_____

_____

_____

_____

_____

_____
_____
_____
_____
_____
_____
_____
_____
_____
_____
_____
_____
_____

WINS:

_____
_____
_____
_____
_____
_____
_____
_____
_____
_____
_____
_____
_____
_____

Week 4

TO DO:

- ☐ Write Introduction
- ☐ Write Chapter 1&2
- ☐ Write Chapter 3&4

NOTES:

_____
_____
_____
_____
_____
_____
_____
_____
_____
_____
_____
_____
_____
_____
_____
_____
_____
_____
_____
_____

_____
_____
_____
_____
_____
_____
_____
_____
_____
_____
_____
_____
_____
_____

WINS:

_____
_____
_____
_____
_____
_____
_____
_____
_____
_____
_____
_____
_____
_____

TO DO:

- ☐ Write Chapter 5&6
- ☐ Write Chapter 7&8
- ☐ Write Chapter 9&10

NOTES:

_____
_____
_____
_____
_____
_____
_____
_____
_____
_____
_____
_____
_____
_____
_____
_____
_____
_____

_____
_____
_____
_____
_____
_____
_____
_____
_____
_____
_____
_____
_____
_____

WINS:

_____
_____
_____
_____
_____
_____
_____
_____
_____
_____
_____
_____
_____
_____

Week 6

TO DO:

- ☐ Analyze Content
- ☐ Front Book Content
- ☐ Back Book Content

NOTES:

_____

_____

_____

_____

_____

_____

_____

_____

_____

_____

_____

_____

_____

_____

_____

_____

_____

_____

_____

_____

_____

_____

_____

_____

_____

_____

_____

_____

_____

_____

_____

_____

_____

WINS:

_____

_____

_____

_____

_____

_____

_____

_____

_____

_____

_____

_____

TO DO:

☐ First Edits

☐ Second Edits

☐ Third & Final Edits

NOTES:

_____

_____

_____

_____

_____

_____

_____

_____

_____

_____

_____

_____

_____

_____

_____

_____

_____

_____

_____
_____
_____
_____
_____
_____
_____
_____
_____
_____
_____
_____
_____

WINS:

_____
_____
_____
_____
_____
_____
_____
_____
_____
_____
_____
_____
_____

TO DO:

- ☐ Pre-formatting Tasks & Arrange Content
- ☐ Formatting Adjustments
- ☐ Add Personal Touch

NOTES:

_____

_____

_____

_____

_____

_____

_____

_____

_____

_____

_____

_____

_____

_____

_____

_____

_____

_____

_____

_____

_____
_____
_____
_____
_____
_____
_____
_____
_____
_____
_____
_____
_____
_____

WINS:

_____
_____
_____
_____
_____
_____
_____
_____
_____
_____
_____
_____
_____

Week 9

TO DO:

☐ Final Formatting Checks

☐ Clarity on cover & content

☐ Hire Graphic Designer

NOTES:

_____

_____

_____

_____

_____

_____

_____

_____

_____

_____

_____

_____

_____

_____

_____

_____

_____

_____

_____
_____
_____
_____
_____
_____
_____
_____
_____
_____
_____
_____
_____
_____

WINS:

_____
_____
_____
_____
_____
_____
_____
_____
_____
_____
_____
_____
_____

TO DO:

- ☐ Final Formatting Checks
- ☐ Clarity on cover & content
- ☐ Hire Graphic Designer

NOTES:

_____

_____

_____

_____

_____

_____

_____

_____

_____

_____

_____

_____

_____

_____

_____

_____

_____

_____

_____

_____

_____

_____

_____

_____

_____

_____

_____

_____

_____

_____

_____

_____

_____

WINS:

_____

_____

_____

_____

_____

_____

_____

_____

_____

_____

_____

_____

_____

Week 10

TO DO:

☐ Manage Design Process

☐ Finalize Cover

☐ Pre-Load Activities

NOTES:

_____

_____

_____

_____

_____

_____

_____

_____

_____

_____

_____

_____

_____

_____

_____

_____

_____

_____

_____

_____
_____
_____
_____
_____
_____
_____
_____
_____
_____
_____
_____
_____
_____

WINS:

_____
_____
_____
_____
_____
_____
_____
_____
_____
_____
_____
_____
_____
_____
_____

TO DO:

- ☐ Create Publish Content
- ☐ Upload Book
- ☐ Request Proof Book

NOTES:

_____

_____

_____

_____

_____

_____

_____

_____

_____

_____

_____

_____

_____

_____

_____

_____

_____

_____

_____

_____

_____
_____
_____
_____
_____
_____
_____
_____
_____
_____
_____
_____

WINS:

_____
_____
_____
_____
_____
_____
_____
_____
_____
_____
_____
_____
_____

TO DO:

- ☐ Create Author's Profile
- ☐ Finalizing Publishing
- ☐ Launch Book

NOTES:

_____

_____

_____

_____

_____

_____

_____

_____

_____

_____

_____

_____

_____

_____

_____

_____

_____

_____

_____

_____
_____
_____
_____
_____
_____
_____
_____
_____
_____
_____
_____
_____

WINS:

_____
_____
_____
_____
_____
_____
_____
_____
_____
_____
_____
_____

Resources

KDP

Owned by Amazon, KDP is a self-publishing platform is #1 choice of DIY authors. It is free to create an account and if you choose not to buy an ISBN, they will assign one to you. They will publish your book to Amazon globally and other distribution channels.

Temi

An artificial intelligence software used to transcribe audio and video content. You can dictate your book and use this software to transcribe it in minutes.

Grammarly

The artificial intelligence software of editors, Grammarly allows you correct critical and advanced grammatical issues with your manuscript. You install it on Word or use the web version.

Bowker Identifier Services

This is only official US ISBN Agency and where you would buy the ISBN for your book if you do not want the free one from KDP.

Kindle Create

Created by KDP, Kindle Create is a formatting software for kindle books. You can download it on your computer an import your eBook manuscript for automated formatting.

Canva

An online graphic design software, Canva is super easy to use and if you possess the creativity you can design your book cover with it.

Pen to Publish

The Pen to Publish website has tons of resources for DIY author including, writing, publishing, and marketing classes, digital downloads, and services.

About the Author

Grace is a woman of God, who is passionate about her Christian walk, her marriage, and being a mom. She uses her life experiences to author books to help parents of autistic kids and Christian women. To date, Grace has authored 8 titles and is an Amazon Best Selling Author of the book "My Son has Autism" and "Still Have Joy".

An international ghostwriter and book coach, Grace is an online entrepreneur who helps others to turn what they know into books and other income generating products. Her company Pen to Publish teaches DIY authors how to write and publish like a pro and on a tight budget. Grace has authored a number of courses and digital resources on self-publishing and this book is the first of her printed work on the topic.

She considers her gift of creativity, content generation, and writing to be of God and is committed to using those gifts to advance the Kingdom of God. In 2019, Grace launched Publishing Disciples, a coaching program to help Christian authors become disciples of the Word through publishing.

In the last year, Grace has authored *"The Word is My Light"* Bible Study Notebook, and the *"In Everything Pray"* prayer journal. The two published works represent projects that the Holy Spirit revealed to Grace in her own worship time. Both books have encouraged others to be more active participants in their Christian walk.

She is also the visionary author and compiler of the Anthology *"Still Have Joy"* - launched in December 2018, this collaborative work became an Amazon Best Seller and #1 Hot New Release. Grace is currently working on a second collaboration - *"When God Says No"*

As a mother of three autistic kids, Grace is an autism advocate who is passionate about teaching parents how to cope on their journey. She is also in the process of establishing a ministry that is close to her heart "Fellowship with Autism." Her goal is to help churches to create a worship experience that is welcoming to individuals of the autism community.

Her published contribution to the autism community includes, *"My Son has Autism"*, *"Autism FAQ"*, and *"Celebrate Everyday"* journal. She is currently working on her next autism book - *"Autism Happens."*

You can contact Grace at:

authorgracemariebrown@gmail.com
contact@pentopublish.com
gracetheghostwriter@gmail.com